THIS WORKBOOK BELONGS TO:

_____

Welcome,
Fellow Lovescaper!

In this workbook, you will find a personal space to work on your Lovescaping skills. You can think of it as a guide and a journal for you to learn, take action and reflect on your practice of the pillars of Lovescaping. We encourage you to be creative and make this workbook your own by using your unique and preferred communication style, whether it's through writing, scribbling, drawing, poetry, doodling, etc. You can also include questions you may have that come up as you put these pillars into practice!

Examples of communication styles you can use in your workbook:

- WRITING
- DRAWING
- POETRY
- DOODLING

TABLE OF CONTENTS

01 GLOSSARY OF TERMS

02 HOW TO USE THIS WORKBOOK

04	HUMILITY	**24**	COMPASSION	**44**	SOLIDARITY
08	EMPATHY	**28**	PATIENCE	**48**	LIBERATION
12	RESPECT	**32**	HONESTY	**52**	GRATITUDE
16	COMMUNICATION	**36**	VULNERABILITY	**56**	FORGIVENESS
20	CARE	**40**	TRUST	**60**	HOPE

GLOSSARY OF TERMS

Definition: the meaning and description of the Lovescaping pillar at the beginning of each section.

Lovescaper: a person who practices all 15 pillars of Lovescaping.

Pillar of Lovescaping: one of the key components and elements to practice love in action. There are 15 in total.

Objectives: the desired goals or learning outcomes for each of the pillars.

Practice: a section where you can put that pillar into practice by working through a scenario.

Reflection: a space where you can think deeply and reflect on your practice of the pillar.

Self-Evaluation: a space where you can assess yourself and take responsibility for your practice of the pillar.

SMART Goal: when setting goals for your life, remember to make them SMART! This will make it more likely for you to accomplish them:

- **Specific**: Make your goal as detailed and specific as possible.
- **Measurable**: Make sure you'll be able to quantify or measure your goal.
- **Actionable**: make sure there are specific actions you can take to achieve your goal.
- **Realistic**: Make sure your goal is something you can actually do; that's why it needs to be realistic.
- **Time-Bound**: Make sure your goal has a specific time frame or deadline.

HOW TO USE THIS
WORKBOOK

This workbook is divided into 15 chapters that correspond to the 15 pillars of Lovescaping. You will find under each "Pillar of the Week" the same format and activities to work through. The goal is for you to use the workbook to reflect, practice and solidify what you're learning at school with Lovescaping. Remember to make this workbook your own and be creative! Under each chapter you will find:

PILLAR OF THE WEEK

In this workbook, you will find activities to practice and review all 15 pillars of Lovescaping. The goal is for you to work on the pillar that you are learning about at school.

OBJECTIVES

The desired goals or learning outcomes for the pillar of the week.

DEFINITION

Review the definition of the Lovescaping pillar and a few examples.

IN YOUR OWN WORDS

Practice giving that pillar your own definition. Remember that you are free to write, draw, or express your idea however you want.

PRACTICE

There is a scenario for each pillar where you have to work through a particular situation and decide how you would practice that pillar.

QUESTIONS

You will be able to write any questions/comments you may have to bring to school and ask your Lovescaping teacher.

GOAL SETTING

You will set your own SMART goal for the week to practice that pillar in your life.

REFLECTION & SELF-EVALUATION

You will answer some questions, reflect on your SMART goal and think about how you can improve.

You will be able to reflect on the relationship between and among all the pillars of Lovescaping.

PILLAR OF THE WEEK
HUMILITY

Objectives

- Define humility in your own words.
- Set a goal for practicing humility this week.
- Reflect on the importance of putting humility into practice.
- Reflect on why humility is one of the pillars of Lovescaping.
- Take Action! Share how you practiced humility this week.

Definition

Humility is understanding that you are not above or below others, better or worse than others, but rather, you see yourself as a human being on the same plain, just different. When we practice humility, we understand that we do not know everything, open ourselves to learning, admit our mistakes, and accept others. When you practice humility, you are humble, and you are free from pride or arrogance. Examples of Humility:

- You listen to others and try to understand them
- You admit mistakes
- You have an open mind
- You embrace differences
- You are open to learning from new ideas
- You are patient
- You take responsibility

PILLAR OF THE WEEK
HUMILITY

Questions
Use this section to write down any questions or thoughts you have to bring back to your Lovescaping teacher next session.

_____

_____

_____

_____

Goal setting
What is one SMART goal you will set this week to practice **humility**?

Example: This week, I will practice humility by spending 15 minutes every day listening to the "This Teenage Life" podcast to learn about different perspectives and experiences from teenagers around the country.

My goal for practicing humility this week:

Is your goal SMART?
- [ ] Specific
- [ ] Measurable
- [ ] Actionable
- [ ] Realistic
- [ ] Time-bound

In your own words | How can you define humility in your own words? What does humility mean or look like for you?

Practice | Scenario: you had a fight with your friend and said mean, hurtful things to them that you later regretted. How can you practice humility in this situation?

_____

Reflection & Self-Evaluation

Did you accomplish your goal?   YES   NO
Why or why not?

Are you committed to being a Lovescaper?   YES   NO
Write two actions for improving and practicing humility from now on:

1.

2.

Why do you think humility is one of the pillars of Lovescaping?

PILLAR OF THE WEEK
EMPATHY

Objectives

- Define empathy in your own words.
- Set a goal for practicing empathy this week.
- Reflect on the importance of putting empathy into practice.
- Reflect on why empathy is one of the pillars of Lovescaping.
- Take Action! Share how you practiced empathy this week.

Definition

Empathy is the ability to understand and share the feelings of another person. It means putting yourself in someone else's shoes to see how things look and feel from someone's situation or perspective. Here are some questions you can ask yourself and work on to build your empathy skills: Can I identify the emotions in others? What are they communicating with their words and body language? How would I feel if it was me? What can I say to show that I care? You are empathetic when you understand and share the feelings of another person. Examples of Empathy:

- You listen deeply with the goal of understanding and not responding
- You can identify the emotions in another person
- You support and care about others
- You don't judge
- You show kindness

PILLAR OF THE WEEK
EMPATHY

Questions | Use this section to write down any questions or thoughts you have to bring back to your Lovescaping teacher next session.

_____
_____
_____
_____

Goal setting | What is one SMART goal you will set this week to practice **empathy**?

Example: This week, I will practice empathy by attending the "welcome new students from around the world" event on Wednesday after-school to listen to my new classmate's stories, understand their different backgrounds, and learn about where they came from.

My goal for practicing empathy this week:

Is your goal SMART?
- ☐ Specific
- ☐ Measurable
- ☐ Actionable
- ☐ Realistic
- ☐ Time-bound

In your own words | How can you define empathy in your own words? What does empathy mean or look like for you?

Practice | Scenario: your friend shares that his girlfriend broke up with him and feels sad and upset. How can you practice empathy in this situation?

_____

Reflection & Self-Evaluation

Did you accomplish your goal?   YES   NO
Why or why not?

Are you committed to being a Lovescaper?   YES   NO
Write two actions for improving and practicing empathy from now on:

1

2

Why do you think empathy is one of the pillars of Lovescaping?

PILLAR OF THE WEEK
RESPECT

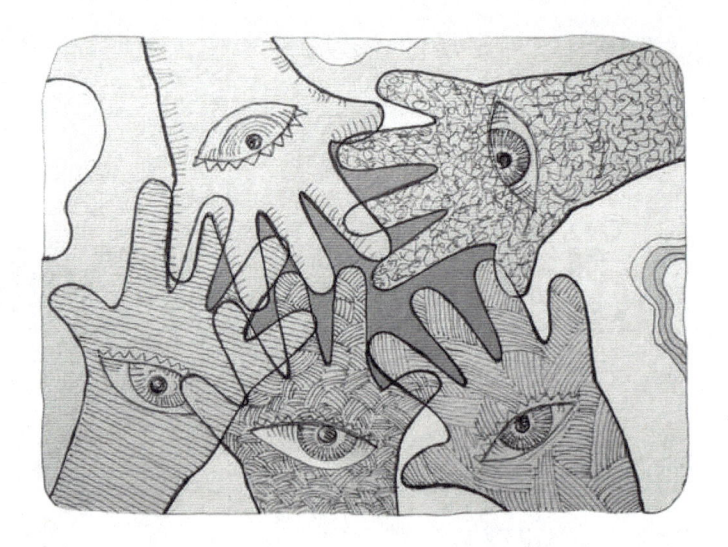

Objectives

- Define respect in your own words.
- Set a goal for practicing respect this week.
- Reflect on the importance of putting respect into practice.
- Reflect on why respect is one of the pillars of Lovescaping.
- Take Action! Share how you practiced respect this week.

Definition

Respect is valuing and accepting ourselves and others, treating one another with dignity. We respect when we give value, listen and recognize another person's voice, point of view, and lived experience. We show respect with our words, body language, and actions. When we respect, we accept people for who they are, without judging them or trying to change them. Examples of Respect:

- You listen to someone when they are talking
- You don't interrupt
- You wait for your turn patiently
- You use words such as "please" and "thank you"
- You treat others the way you want to be treated
- You communicate using "I" messages
- You make eye contact
- You use your words and body language to show that you are paying attention

PILLAR OF THE WEEK
RESPECT

Questions
Use this section to write down any questions or thoughts you have to bring back to your Lovescaping teacher next session.

_____

_____

_____

_____

Goal setting
What is one SMART goal you will set this week to practice **respect**?

Example: This week, I will practice respect with my little brother every evening. I will put my phone away for 20 minutes to ask him questions about his day, listen to him with interest, make eye contact and ask follow-up questions.

My goal for practicing respect this week:

Is your goal SMART?
- ☐ Specific
- ☐ Measurable
- ☐ Actionable
- ☐ Realistic
- ☐ Time-bound

In your own words | How can you define respect in your own words? What does respect mean or look like for you?

Practice | Scenario: one of your teachers said something that felt disrespectful to you. How can you practice respect in this situation?

_____

Reflection & Self-Evaluation

Did you accomplish your goal? YES   NO
Why or why not?

Are you committed to being a Lovescaper? YES   NO
Write two actions for improving and practicing respect from now on:

1.

2.

Why do you think respect is one of the pillars of Lovescaping?

PILLAR OF THE WEEK
COMMUNICATION

Objectives

- Define communication in your own words.
- Set a goal for practicing communication this week.
- Reflect on the importance of putting communication into practice.
- Reflect on why communication is one of the pillars of Lovescaping.
- Take Action! Share how you practiced communication this week.

Definition

Communication is the process by which we transmit our thoughts, feelings, and emotions through different mediums. We constantly communicate, exchanging information, and addressing each other in verbal and non-verbal ways. Communication is the basis of any relationship. Our ability to communicate allows us to survive, grow, and develop. Examples of Communication:

- You make eye contact when speaking to others
- You listen to others respectfully
- You ask questions when you don't understand something
- You write or text with others
- You use pictures or emojis to express yourself
- You use words to resolve conflict
- You use "I' messages to communicate your needs
- You use your body language

PILLAR OF THE WEEK
COMMUNICATION

Questions |
Use this section to write down any questions or thoughts you have to bring back to your Lovescaping teacher next session.

_____
_____
_____
_____

Goal setting | What is one SMART goal you will set this week to practice **communication**?

Example: This week, I will practice communication by raising my hand in class at least once during Math class. I will ask my teacher questions about the formulas that I don't understand.

My goal for practicing communication this week:

Is your goal SMART?
- ☐ Specific
- ☐ Measurable
- ☐ Actionable
- ☐ Realistic
- ☐ Time-bound

In your own words | How can you define communication in your own words? What does communication mean or look like for you?

Practice | Scenario: you need some time alone, but you're scared to tell your friends because they take it personally and think it's because you don't like them anymore. How can you communicate your needs to them?

_____

Reflection & Self-Evaluation

Did you accomplish your goal?   YES   NO
Why or why not?

Are you committed to being a Lovescaper?   YES   NO
Write two actions for improving and practicing communication from now on:

1

2

Why do you think communication is one of the pillars of Lovescaping?

PILLAR OF THE WEEK
CARE

Objectives

- Define care in your own words.
- Set a goal for practicing care this week.
- Reflect on the importance of putting care into practice.
- Reflect on why care is one of the pillars of Lovescaping.
- Take Action! Share how you practiced care this week.

Definition

Care is giving time and attention to and looking after things or people that matter to us with kindness and affection. We show that we care about others by being consistent, reliable, and trustworthy. The most precious gift we can give someone to show that we care is our time. Self-Care is directing that attention, kindness and affection towards ourselves. Self-Care is any activity you do to take care of your mental, physical, and emotional health. Examples of Care:

- You spend quality time with people you love
- You help people when they need it
- You keep your word: if you make a promise, you own it; if you make a commitment, you stick to it
- You call friends and family who are far away
- You hug the people you love
- You do an act of kindness for someone else
- You eat healthy foods and exercise regularly

PILLAR OF THE WEEK
CARE

Questions |
Use this section to write down any questions or thoughts you have to bring back to your Lovescaping teacher next session.

_____
_____
_____
_____

Goal setting | What is one SMART goal you will set this week to practice **care**?

Example: This week, I will practice self-care by listening to a 10-minute guided meditation every night before going to bed.

My goal for practicing care this week:

Is your goal SMART?
- [ ] Specific
- [ ] Measurable
- [ ] Actionable
- [ ] Realistic
- [ ] Time-bound

In your own words | How can you define care in your own words? What does care mean or look like for you?

Practice | Scenario: your mother is working three jobs, and you see how tired she is every time she gets home. How can you practice care in this situation?

_____

Reflection & Self-Evaluation

Did you accomplish your goal?   YES   NO
Why or why not?

Are you committed to being a Lovescaper?   YES   NO
Write two actions for improving and practicing care and self-care from now on:

1

2

Why do you think care is one of the pillars of Lovescaping?

PILLAR OF THE WEEK
COMPASSION

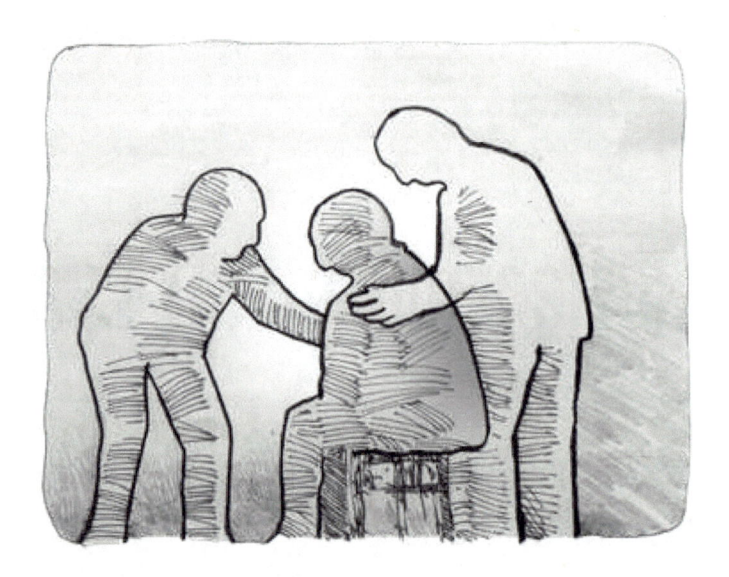

Objectives

- Define compassion in your own words.
- Set a goal for practicing compassion this week.
- Reflect on the importance of putting compassion into practice.
- Reflect on why compassion is one of the pillars of Lovescaping.
- Take Action! Share how you practiced compassion this week.

Definition

Compassion means being able to share other people's suffering and feel with them. Being compassionate helps alleviate the suffering of those around us because we share it. When we are compassionate, we are letting others know they are not alone in their grief, that we care about them and that we are there to support them. Compassion is the foundation of humanity. When we lose our compassion, we risk losing our humanity. When we don't care about the suffering of others, it's easy to become indifferent and do nothing to help make things better. Compassion is necessary to take action and help heal our world! Examples of Compassion:

- You notice when others are feeling sad
- You reach out and provide support when others are sad
- You have felt sad when others are sad too
- You act when someone is being mistreated
- You listen to others when they are going through a difficult time

PILLAR OF THE WEEK
COMPASSION

Questions
Use this section to write down any questions or thoughts you have to bring back to your Lovescaping teacher next session.

Goal setting
What is one SMART goal you will set this week to practice **compassion**?

Example: This week, I will practice compassion by paying close attention to my classmates and noticing at least two who seem to be sad or worried and asking them if they are okay and what I can do to support them.

My goal for practicing compassion this week:

Is your goal SMART?
- [ ] Specific
- [ ] Measurable
- [ ] Actionable
- [ ] Realistic
- [ ] Time-bound

In your own words | How can you define compassion in your own words? What does compassion mean or look like for you?

Practice | Scenario: your teacher shares with you that she's grieving because she just lost her mother. How can you practice compassion in this situation?

_____

Reflection & Self-Evaluation

Did you accomplish your goal?   YES   NO
Why or why not?

Are you committed to being a Lovescaper?   YES   NO
Write two actions for improving and practicing compassion from now on:

1

2

Why do you think compassion is one of the pillars of Lovescaping?

PILLAR OF THE WEEK
PATIENCE

Objectives

- Define patience in your own words.
- Set a goal for practicing patience this week.
- Reflect on the importance of putting patience into practice.
- Reflect on why patience is one of the pillars of Lovescaping.
- Take Action! Share how you practiced patience this week.

Definition

Patience is allowing time for things to happen and develop without becoming agitated, upset, or losing our temper. The key to patience is realizing that most things that are important in this world require time. It takes time to develop trust, to learn, to understand, and ultimately to love. When you are patient, you understand and value the time that it takes to work on yourself, on relationships, on learning, and growing. Having patience helps you persevere and not give up. Examples of Patience:

- You wait for your turn to speak
- You don't get frustrated with others
- You have a good attitude while waiting for something
- You don't give up, and you try again
- You keep working towards your goals
- You are empathetic with others
- You put in the time it takes to learn new things

PILLAR OF THE WEEK
PATIENCE

Questions |
Use this section to write down any questions or thoughts you have to bring back to your Lovescaping teacher next session.

_____
_____
_____
_____

Goal setting | What is one SMART goal you will set this week to practice **patience**?

Example: This week, I will practice patience by doing a breathing exercise while doing my homework every night: every time I get stuck, instead of throwing my notebook and getting angry, I will close my eyes and do the square breathing exercise.

My goal for practicing patience this week:

Is your goal SMART?
- ☐ Specific
- ☐ Measurable
- ☐ Actionable
- ☐ Realistic
- ☐ Time-bound

In your own words | How can you define patience in your own words? What does patience mean or look like for you?

Practice | Scenario: in the past, you would always lose your patience with your little brother and yell at him whenever he asked you to play with him. How can you practice patience in this situation?

_____

Reflection & Self-Evaluation

Did you accomplish your goal?   YES   NO
Why or why not?

Are you committed to being a Lovescaper?   YES   NO
Write two actions for improving and practicing patience from now on:

1

2

Why do you think patience is one of the pillars of Lovescaping?

PILLAR OF THE WEEK
HONESTY

Objectives

- Define honesty in your own words.
- Set a goal for practicing honesty this week.
- Reflect on the importance of putting honesty into practice.
- Reflect on why honesty is one of the pillars of Lovescaping.
- Take Action! Share how you practiced honesty this week.

Definition

Honesty is being truthful, open, and transparent. Honesty means speaking our truth to others, expressing our feelings, emotions, fears, dreams, doubts, and experiences. Honesty allows us to build authentic relationships based on our true selves. Being honest can be very difficult; it can even hurt at times, but it is necessary to build a solid relationship based on trust. Examples of Honesty:

- You tell the truth, even when it's hard
- You behave with integrity: you do the right thing when no one is watching
- You share how you really feel and what you really think
- You are honest with yourself and seek help if you need it
- You are respectful when you communicate honestly with others
- You take responsibility for your actions
- You stick to your promises and commitments
- You admit and acknowledge your lies

PILLAR OF THE WEEK
HONESTY

Questions
Use this section to write down any questions or thoughts you have to bring back to your Lovescaping teacher next session.

_____

_____

_____

_____

Goal setting
What is one SMART goal you will set this week to practice **honesty**?

Example: This week, I will practice honesty by talking to my teacher on Wednesday after class and telling her that sometimes when I fall asleep in class, it's not because I'm lazy or disrespectful, but because I have a job after-school. Sometimes I don't get enough sleep at night.

My goal for practicing honesty this week:

Is your goal SMART?
- [ ] Specific
- [ ] Measurable
- [ ] Actionable
- [ ] Realistic
- [ ] Time-bound

In your own words | How can you define honesty in your own words? What does honesty mean or look like for you?

Practice | Scenario: you are out with your friends, and it's 9:45pm. You have a 10pm curfew, and you know your mom is waiting and needs to wake up very early to go to work. How can you practice honesty in this situation?

_____

Reflection & Self-Evaluation

Did you accomplish your goal?   YES   NO
Why or why not?

Are you committed to being a Lovescaper?   YES   NO
Write two actions for improving and practicing honesty from now on:

1.

2.

Why do you think honesty is one of the pillars of Lovescaping?

PILLAR OF THE WEEK
VULNERABILITY

Objectives

- Define vulnerability in your own words.
- Set a goal for practicing vulnerability this week.
- Reflect on the importance of putting vulnerability into practice.
- Reflect on why vulnerability is one of the pillars of Lovescaping.
- Take Action! Share how you practiced vulnerability this week.

Definition

Vulnerability is uncertainty, risk and emotional exposure. When we are vulnerable, we open our hearts and show our true selves. Vulnerability is courageous, and when we learn to be vulnerable with one another, we develop honesty, trust and build stronger relationships. Examples of Vulnerability:

- You express and share all your feelings
- You share your pain and insecurities
- You take risks
- You are okay with uncertainty
- You believe that expressing all your emotions is brave
- You understand that nobody is perfect
- You open up about the things that you are afraid of

PILLAR OF THE WEEK
VULNERABILITY

Questions |
Use this section to write down any questions or thoughts you have to bring back to your Lovescaping teacher next session.

Goal setting | What is one SMART goal you will set this week to practice **vulnerability**?

Example: This week, I will practice vulnerability by getting together with my best friend over the weekend and sharing with him an experience that made me feel ashamed and insecure.

My goal for practicing vulnerability this week:

Is your goal SMART?
- [ ] Specific
- [ ] Measurable
- [ ] Actionable
- [ ] Realistic
- [ ] Time-bound

In your own words | How can you define vulnerability in your own words? What does vulnerability mean or look like for you?

Practice | Scenario: you are struggling a lot with some family problems and feel scared and lonely. Your favorite teacher asks you if you are okay. How can you practice vulnerability in this situation?

___

Reflection & Self-Evaluation

Did you accomplish your goal?   YES   NO
Why or why not?

Are you committed to being a Lovescaper?   YES   NO
Write two actions for improving and practicing vulnerability from now on:

1.

2.

Why do you think vulnerability is one of the pillars of Lovescaping?

PILLAR OF THE WEEK
TRUST

Objectives

- Define trust in your own words.
- Set a goal for practicing trust this week.
- Reflect on the importance of putting trust into practice.
- Reflect on why trust is one of the pillars of Lovescaping.
- Take Action! Share how you practiced trust this week.

Definition

Trust is the ability to believe sincerely in someone or something. It requires us to be vulnerable and honest and to let go of fear. Developing trust takes time. Trust is the consequence of being honest, caring, vulnerable, and communicative. Examples of Trust:

- You keep your promises
- You are reliable
- You follow through with your commitments
- You keep secrets
- You don't give in to peer pressure
- You are honest
- You have integrity
- You are consistent

PILLAR OF THE WEEK
TRUST

Questions
Use this section to write down any questions or thoughts you have to bring back to your Lovescaping teacher next session.

_____
_____
_____
_____

Goal setting
What is one SMART goal you will set this week to practice **trust**?

Example: This week, I will practice trust by doing all my house chores every day after-school and letting my family know I kept my commitment.

My goal for practicing trust this week:

Is your goal SMART?
- [ ] Specific
- [ ] Measurable
- [ ] Actionable
- [ ] Realistic
- [ ] Time-bound

In your own words | How can you define trust in your own words? What does trust mean or look like for you?

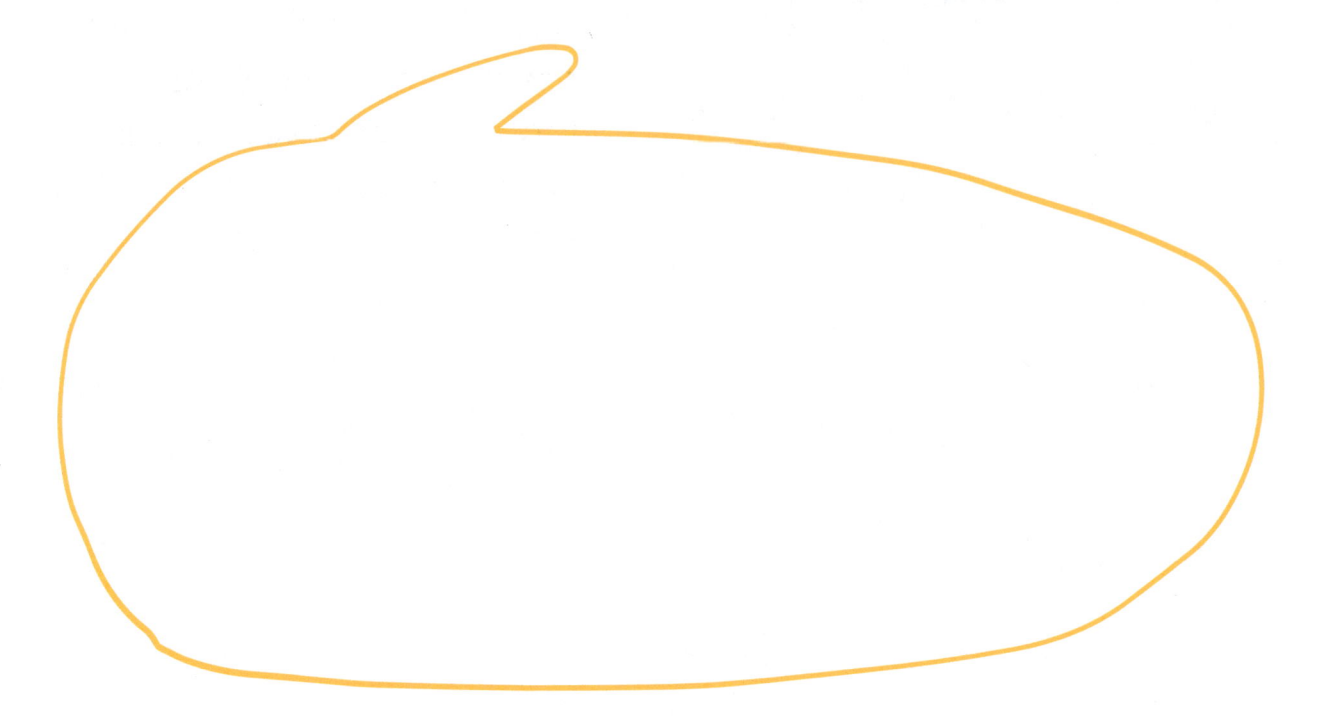

Practice | Scenario: your best friend tells you a secret. How can you practice trust in this situation?

Reflection & Self-Evaluation

Did you accomplish your goal?   YES   NO
Why or why not?

Are you committed to being a Lovescaper?   YES   NO
Write two actions for improving and practicing trust from now on:

1.

2.

Why do you think trust is one of the pillars of Lovescaping?

PILLAR OF THE WEEK
SOLIDARITY

Objectives

- Define solidarity in your own words.
- Set a goal for practicing solidarity this week.
- Reflect on the importance of putting solidarity into practice.
- Reflect on why solidarity is one of the pillars of Lovescaping.
- Take Action! Share how you practiced solidarity this week.

Definition

Solidarity is caring about the wellbeing of others and uniting to achieve a common goal. You are solidary when you give your time, support and care to others. When we are solidary, we support a cause even if it doesn't directly affect us. Solidarity is about realizing that we are all interconnected, so we stand together and support the wellbeing and liberation of others. Examples of Solidarity:

- You care about others
- You notice when someone is struggling and give your helping hand
- You support groups you are not a part of
- You volunteer and give your time to help
- You use your voice to provide support or assistance to people who need it
- You believe we all have a responsibility to make sure everyone in our community is cared for

PILLAR OF THE WEEK
SOLIDARITY

Questions

Use this section to write down any questions or thoughts you have to bring back to your Lovescaping teacher next session.

_____

_____

_____

_____

Goal setting

What is one SMART goal you will set this week to practice **solidarity**?

Example: This week, I will practice solidarity by organizing a group of friends to pick up the trash in our neighborhood on Saturday morning and start a social media campaign to bring awareness about the problem and teach neighbors about the importance of taking care of our community.

My goal for practicing solidarity this week:

Is your goal SMART?
- ☐ Specific
- ☐ Measurable
- ☐ Actionable
- ☐ Realistic
- ☐ Time-bound

In your own words | How can you define solidarity in your own words? What does solidarity mean or look like for you?

Practice | Scenario: one of your classmates was a victim of a racist attack in the neighborhood. How can you practice solidarity in this situation?

Reflection & Self-Evaluation

Did you accomplish your goal?   YES   NO
Why or why not?

Are you committed to being a Lovescaper?   YES   NO
Write two actions for improving and practicing solidarity from now on:

1

2

Why do you think solidarity is one of the pillars of Lovescaping?

PILLAR OF THE WEEK
LIBERATION

Objectives

- Define liberation in your own words.
- Set a goal for practicing liberation this week.
- Reflect on the importance of putting liberation into practice.
- Reflect on why liberation is one of the pillars of Lovescaping.
- Take Action! Share how you practiced liberation this week.

Definition

Liberation is the act of setting free. Love is liberating, which means it sets free. We practice liberation through our actions of love, because we learn to respect each other's humanity. The act of loving is an act of freedom, because it has no boundaries, and it doesn't oppress or discriminate. Love liberates because it trusts, and it sets the people we love free. In the practice of love, we respect the individuality and freedom of every human being and we learn that our liberation is tied to each other's. Our liberation comes with great responsibility to practice it alongside the other pillars of Lovescaping so that we don't misuse it to harm others. Examples of Liberation:

- You want everyone to have the same rights
- You speak up if you see an act of injustice
- You care when others are not being treated fairly, and you become an ally to support communities that you are not a part of
- You believe everybody should be treated fairly

PILLAR OF THE WEEK
LIBERATION

Questions
Use this section to write down any questions or thoughts you have to bring back to your Lovescaping teacher next session.

___

Goal setting
What is one SMART goal you will set this week to practice **liberation**?

Example: This week, I will practice liberation by watching a 2-hour documentary on Friday night about the history and legacy of slavery in the United States and discussing what I learned with my friends and teacher the following week.

My goal for practicing liberation this week:

Is your goal SMART?
- [ ] Specific
- [ ] Measurable
- [ ] Actionable
- [ ] Realistic
- [ ] Time-bound

In your own words | How can you define liberation in your own words? What does liberation mean or look like for you?

Practice | Scenario: a group of students in special education are asking for more inclusion in school activities and better infrastructure and accessibility at the school, like having ramps for wheelchairs. How can you practice liberation in this situation?

_____

Reflection & Self-Evaluation

Did you accomplish your goal?   YES   NO
Why or why not?

Are you committed to being a Lovescaper?   YES   NO
Write two actions for improving and practicing liberation from now on:

①

②

Why do you think liberation is one of the pillars of Lovescaping?

PILLAR OF THE WEEK
GRATITUDE

Objectives

- Define gratitude in your own words.
- Set a goal for practicing gratitude this week.
- Reflect on the importance of putting gratitude into practice.
- Reflect on why gratitude is one of the pillars of Lovescaping.
- Take Action! Share how you practiced gratitude this week.

Definition

Gratitude is a sense of thankfulness or appreciation for the good in our lives. To be grateful means to acknowledge other people's actions with kindness, to feel a sense of appreciation and thankfulness for what we are, for what we do, for what we receive and for what we have. It goes beyond saying "Thank you," to actually feeling it. When we start to acknowledge all the acts of kindness around us and to actively engage in reminding ourselves of everything that we can be grateful for, we begin to cultivate appreciation for our lives, for all the simple things that we often take for granted. Examples of Gratitude:

- You say thank you
- You express gratitude regularly to people in your life
- You appreciate all the things others do for you
- You keep a gratitude journal
- You look for the good in your life
- You don't compare yourself to others

PILLAR OF THE WEEK
GRATITUDE

Questions

Use this section to write down any questions or thoughts you have to bring back to your Lovescaping teacher next session.

_____

_____

_____

_____

Goal setting | What is one SMART goal you will set this week to practice **gratitude**?

Example: This week, I will practice gratitude by writing down in my journal one thing that I'm grateful for when I wake up every day of the week.

My goal for practicing gratitude this week:

Is your goal SMART?
- [ ] Specific
- [ ] Measurable
- [ ] Actionable
- [ ] Realistic
- [ ] Time-bound

In your own words | How can you define gratitude in your own words? What does gratitude mean or look like for you?

Practice | Scenario: your school counselor has always been there to support you whenever you needed help. She is leaving your school. How can you practice gratitude in this situation?

_____

Reflection & Self-Evaluation

Did you accomplish your goal?   YES   NO
Why or why not?

Are you committed to being a Lovescaper?   YES   NO
Write two actions for improving and practicing gratitude from now on:

1

2

Why do you think gratitude is one of the pillars of Lovescaping?

PILLAR OF THE WEEK
FORGIVENESS

Objectives

- Define forgiveness in your own words.
- Set a goal for practicing forgiveness this week.
- Reflect on the importance of putting forgiveness into practice.
- Reflect on why forgiveness is one of the pillars of Lovescaping.
- Take Action! Share how you practiced forgiveness this week.

Definition

Forgiveness is being able to let go of the negative emotions that someone or something made us feel, and finding peace within ourselves to forgive others. The process of forgiveness takes time, but in the end, it benefits us, since holding on to anger, resentment, and hatred will only cause us more pain. As imperfect human beings, we all make mistakes and we are all capable of hurting others, many times unintentionally. Being able to forgive others and asking for forgiveness are acts of love, and necessary ones if we want to nurture a relationship. Examples of Forgiveness:

- You are able to forgive others who have harmed you
- You don't hold grudges
- You liberate yourself from negative emotions and find peace
- You forgive but you don't forget
- You don't seek revenge

PILLAR OF THE WEEK
FORGIVENESS

Questions
Use this section to write down any questions or thoughts you have to bring back to your Lovescaping teacher next session.

_____
_____
_____
_____

Goal setting
What is one SMART goal you will set this week to practice **forgiveness**?

Example: This week, I will practice forgiveness by spending two hours over the weekend watching stories about forgiveness on the "The Forgiveness Project" website and reflecting on my own life and writing down in my journal who I haven't been able to forgive and why.

My goal for practicing forgiveness this week:

Is your goal SMART?
- [ ] Specific
- [ ] Measurable
- [ ] Actionable
- [ ] Realistic
- [ ] Time-bound

In your own words | How can you define forgiveness in your own words? What does forgiveness mean or look like for you?

Practice | Scenario: you had a fight with your brother many years ago and haven't seen him since. He recently came to see you to apologize. How can you practice forgiveness in this situation?

_____

Reflection & Self-Evaluation

Did you accomplish your goal? YES NO
Why or why not?

Are you committed to being a Lovescaper? YES NO
Write two actions for improving and practicing forgiveness from now on:

1

2

Why do you think forgiveness is one of the pillars of Lovescaping?

PILLAR OF THE WEEK
HOPE

Objectives

- Define hope in your own words.
- Set a goal for practicing hope this week.
- Reflect on the importance of putting hope into practice.
- Reflect on why hope is one of the pillars of Lovescaping.
- Take Action! Share how you practiced hope this week.

Definition

Hope is the guiding light that carries love through difficult and dark times. Hope means having faith in humanity and in the broader goal of creating a society based on the principles of love. It means believing that things will get better, that situations will improve, that change is possible. Hope is never lost in the pursuit of love, and it is the one pillar that can never, ever fall in our temple. Hope is always strong, holding the structure together and allowing us to rebuild the others. Examples of Hope:

- You believe that change is possible
- You believe that you are capable of achieving your dreams
- You persevere and know that situations can improve
- You have an optimistic view of your future
- You believe you are capable of overcoming obstacles
- You don't give up
- You give encouragement to others when they are feeling low

PILLAR OF THE WEEK
HOPE

Questions |
Use this section to write down any questions or thoughts you have to bring back to your Lovescaping teacher next session.

Goal setting | What is one SMART goal you will set this week to practice **hope**?

Example: This week, I will practice hope by spending 10 minutes every night writing down positive messages and affirmations that I can post around in my room to give me encouragement and hope whenever I'm feeling low.

My goal for practicing hope this week:

Is your goal SMART?

- ☐ Specific
- ☐ Measurable
- ☐ Actionable
- ☐ Realistic
- ☐ Time-bound

In your own words | How can you define hope in your own words? What does hope mean or look like for you?

Practice | Scenario: your mother lost her job and you didn't pass your English exam. You are feeling worried and stressed about your future and your family's. How can you practice hope in this situation?

_____

Reflection & Self-Evaluation

Did you accomplish your goal?   YES   NO
Why or why not?

Are you committed to being a Lovescaper?   YES   NO
Write two actions for improving and practicing hope from now on:

1

2

Why do you think hope is one of the pillars of Lovescaping?

**BE A
LOVESCAPER!**

Made in the USA
Columbia, SC
26 August 2024